The Photography of
John Gutmann: Culture Shock

The Photography of
John Gutmann: Culture Shock

Essay by Sandra S. Phillips

Exhibition organized by Joel Leivick and Bernard Barryte

Merrell Publishers
in association with the
Iris & B. Gerald Cantor Center for Visual Arts at Stanford University

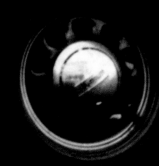

This book accompanies the exhibition
John Gutmann: Culture Shock

Exhibition itinerary:
Iris & B. Gerald Cantor Center for Visual Arts at Stanford University
January 19 – March 26, 2000

Museum of Contemporary Art, Los Angeles
August 12 – November 5, 2000

San Antonio Museum of Art
November 28, 2000 – February 25, 2001

Henry Art Gallery, University of Washington, Seattle
March 13 – May 27, 2001

This exhibition and book have been made possible by generous
support from The Capital Group Companies, Inc.
and The Capital Group Foundation

front cover:
    Self-Portrait, San Francisco 1934 (detail; see pl. 1)
back cover:
    Thanksgiving Service, Camp Roberts, California 1942
    (detail; see pl. 76)
frontispiece:
    "Ham and Eggs," San Francisco 1938 (detail; see pl. 70)
pp. 4–5:
    *Maintenance Worker Moving Down Main Cable of Golden Gate
    Bridge, San Francisco* 1947 (detail; see pl. 8)
pp. 6–7:
    "Yes, Columbus Did Discover America," San Francisco 1938
    (detail; see pl. 74)
pp. 8–9:
    Spotting the Somersaults 1939 (detail; see pl. 36)

First published in 2000 by
Merrell Publishers Limited
42 Southwark Street, London SE1 1UN
in association with the
Iris & B. Gerald Cantor Center for Visual Arts at Stanford University
Stanford, California 94305–5060
USA

Distributed in the USA and Canada by
Rizzoli International Publications, Inc.
through St Martin's Press, 175 Fifth Avenue, New York,
New York 10010

British Library Cataloguing-in-Publication Data:
Phillips, Sandra S., 1945–
    The photography of John Gutmann : culture shock
    1.Gutman, John 2.Photographers – United States – Biography
    3.Photography, Artistic – Exhibitions 4.United States –
    Social conditions – 20th century – Pictorial works
    I.Title
    770.9'2

ISBN 0 85894 097 4 Hardback
ISBN 0 85894 099 0 Paperback

Photographs belong to The Capital Group Companies, Inc.
or The Capital Group Foundation

Edited by Bernard Barryte and Julian Honer
Designed by Maggi Smith

Produced by Merrell Publishers London
Printed and bound in Spain

Contents

Foreword

It gives me great pleasure to present this exhibition of the work of John Gutmann, who was my friend for many years. Our friendship began around a shared passion for African art and continued for over twenty years. Another old friend, Robbie Macfarlane, introduced me to The Capital Group Foundation, where he serves as an advisor and board director. The Foundation and The Capital Group Companies, Inc. have a serious interest in acquiring important works of art for educational purposes. Many works in the Foundation's collection are on loan to Claremont Graduate University and enrich that campus.

In 1993 we presented works by Ansel Adams and Edward Weston from the collections of The Capital Group Companies and The Capital Group Foundation in an exhibition rich in interpretive content. This project led to a deeper relationship. Joel Leivick, Senior Lecturer in Art and Art History and the Cantor Arts Center's honorary curator of photography, began working with The Capital Group on a mutually beneficial program that includes advising them on their photographic acquisitions. Many of these acquisitions have been placed on loan at Stanford for use in exhibitions and teaching. We determined that the best and most interesting course would be to acquire a large body of photographs from a few significant artists whose work focused on the Western United States. Joel and his research assistant, Phillip Prodger, prepared a dossier of several artists, among them John Gutmann. John was enthusiastic that an archive of his most important work might be housed at Stanford. John's initial selections for the collection were reviewed by his friend and assistant, Susan Friedewald, his

dealer, Jeffrey Fraenkel, Bob Egelston, Robbie Macfarlane, Joel, and me. The photographs presented here are the result of that collaboration and have been further strengthened by an insightful essay by Sandra Phillips for this catalogue.

The desire of the Cantor Arts Center and The Capital Group to share these beautiful and historically rich images with a larger audience has resulted in the tour of the exhibition to several other museums. This entire effort has been generously supported by The Capital Group Companies and The Capital Group Foundation, under the visionary leadership of Robert B. Egelston, the Foundation Board, and their curator, Martha W. Williams. We are very grateful to them for their generous and ongoing support.

All the collaborators mentioned above have been instrumental in realizing this project. Our curator, Joel Leivick, and chief curator, Bernard Barryte, have been central to the conceptualization and implementation of the catalogue and exhibition. They have been ably assisted by our registrarial, technical, education, and external relations staff. Credit also goes to our co-publisher, Merrell, for this handsome catalogue.

We deeply regret that our friend John Gutmann died in June 1998 at the age of ninety-three. He was vital and engaged to the end. His extraordinary images, created during a long and productive life, speak volumes about the changes in our world. John's unique vision has enriched us all. We dedicate this catalogue and exhibition to the memory of this unique artist.

Thomas K. Seligman
John & Jill Freidenrich Director
Iris & B. Gerald Cantor Center for Visual Arts at Stanford University

1   John Gutmann, *Tommy Johnson und Liebende in Cabaret Gross, Breslau*, 1925. Ink on paper, 27 x 20 ½ in. Estate of the artist

John Gutmann: Culture Shock

Sandra S. Phillips

I Gutmann's Artistic Origins

John Gutmann was born in the Silesian city of Breslau (now Wrocław, Poland) in 1905 to a wealthy businessman and his wife. The household was typical of middle-class, secular Jews of that time: they identified deeply with German culture and far less with their Jewish ties. Gutmann's father, although prosperous and well connected, had no taste for art. His son, however, pursued a career in art on his own, at a moment when high artistic activity flourished in Germany simultaneously with the emergence of a strong and lively populist culture after World War I. The young Gutmann drew constantly and read avidly. Like many of his contemporaries, he devoured the novels of Karl May, the German author of romantic fiction about the American Indian. Later, Gutmann came to admire the work of such authors as Jack London, Ernest Hemingway, and Theodore Dreiser, though he was never a dedicated student of the American novel. When Gutmann and his contemporaries in Germany thought of America, they imagined cities bristling with skyscrapers, a Wild West with painted Indians, gangsters, and Negro jazz; they were attracted to the myth of American independence, unconventionality, and individuality. As with others of his generation, Gutmann's fantasies were fostered by popular magazines of the time, including the pictorial ones.

As an art student, Gutmann was fortunate to study with the Expressionist artist Otto Müller (1874–1930) at the local academy. Müller was a member of Die Brücke, the so-called "figurative" Expressionists who became associated in Dresden in 1905 and included Ernst Ludwig Kirchner, Emil Nolde, and Erich Heckel. German Expressionist art, especially as practised by members of Die Brücke, was both stylistically daring and deeply identified with a German mythic past. These artists exalted both a primal or primitive expression and the intense spirituality of their Gothic ancestry. Müller was a romantic artist whose strong, rough brushwork obscured a man of delicate sensibility. His most frequent subjects were nude bathers in the open air, and gypsies. Gutmann's interest in exoticism and primitivism was certainly stimulated by his early experience, not only by his contact with Müller, but also through the general Expressionist fascination with African art and "exotic" peoples. When the artist Erich Heckel visited Breslau, Müller showed his good friend a painting Gutmann had made in 1926, in a style similar to fig. 1, of a visiting group of black American performers to the city.

In 1927 Gutmann left his home town to further his artistic studies in the wild, exciting metropolis of Berlin. This city was not only the most important center of high cultural achievement in Germany for art, theater, and literature, but it was also the hub of a lively café and night-life and the

2   John Gutmann, *Chocolate Kiddies*, 1926. Oil on canvas.
Location unknown

center of a prosperous movie industry—all much admired by its artists, and depicted by its painters, including Gutmann himself. Today we recognize Kurt Weill's *The Threepenny Opera* (1928) and Bertolt Brecht's proletarian heroes as important cultural monuments, but they are only part of a larger, richer picture of cosmopolitan life depicted, for instance, in Christopher Isherwood's *Berlin Stories* (1935).[1] The city was a vibrant place, its intensity the consequence of its recent freedom from the authoritarian rule of the Kaiser and the horrors of war. Berlin's deliciously decadent night-life was internationally acclaimed. Expressionist art, Constructivism, and Dadaist tendencies all collided, and, in the 1930s, the New Realist (Neue Sachlichkeit) painters introduced a more somber and strange element in contemporary painting. Gutmann became a connoisseur of it all. The artists of Die Brücke congregated in the city and were supported by dealers important in the history of German modern art: Ernst Cassirer, Alfred Flechtheim, Herwarth Walden, Ferdinand Moeller, and Fritz Gurlitt. Gurlitt had stepped in and offered the artists of Die Brücke a show in 1912 after they resigned from the Neue Secession the previous year. It was Gurlitt, too, who in 1931 gave Gutmann his most important exhibition in Germany, and Moeller offered to show his drawings shortly before he left Germany.

Gutmann was a serious working artist in Berlin. In addition to accumulating academic credentials that would be useful to him when he arrived in the United States, and exhibiting in noteworthy and historically important galleries, he was an artist actively examining the condition of modern life. Gutmann's paintings and drawings are not characteristically Expressionist in the terms of Die Brücke art: they do not have the jagged brushwork, the acid, intense color, or the sense of acute psychological dislocation that characterizes the work of Kirchner, for example. Indeed, before he left Breslau, Gutmann had become familiar with the next generation of artists, the realist painters of the Neue Sachlichkeit, and his work has strong ties to their art. Gutmann's Berlin paintings share some of the subject-matter employed by the older Expressionists, but stylistically and in their sense of ominous social disharmony they have greater affinities to works by Otto Dix and Christian Schad. Gutmann made a series of self-portraits (one with a visual comparison of his face to African sculpture) and paintings that drew on scenes from contemporary life: the circus, the beach, the night-life in Berlin. These pictures are more tonal than coloristic, and there is a sense of emotional isolation in the objects depicted; the space in some is long and distant, and indirectly related to Surrealism (fig. 2).[2]

II Gutmann and the German Popular Press

A number of literary and critical magazines flourished within the context of Berlin's café culture. Probably the most famous publication, the pocket-sized *Der Querschnitt* (*The Profile;* fig. 3), was founded in 1920 by the elegant art dealer Alfred Flechtheim. Unlike more popular magazines, it distinguished itself by a clever drawing on its yellow cover, and included, besides literary essays, witty sketches, satiric drawings, and some well-chosen photographs. These were usually published singly, but sometimes paired to achieve an amusing juxtaposition—placing a László Moholy-Nagy photograph, for instance, beside a comparable folk painting. In 1924 the Ullstein Company, a family corporation of magazines and newspapers, bought *Der Querschnitt* and expanded its circulation.[3] Flechtheim was not the only dealer to combine *belles lettres*, art, and an engagement with Berlin life in his magazine. Albeit briefly, Herwarth Walden also published a magazine—like his gallery, it was called *Der*

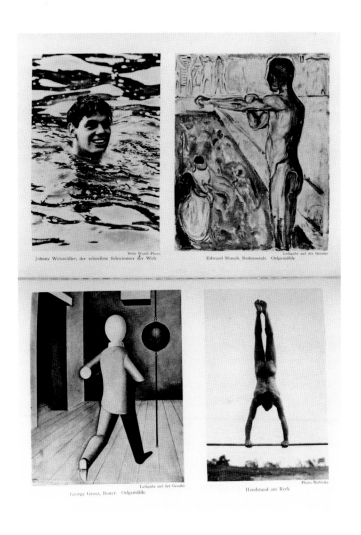

3 *Der Querschnitt*, 6, no. 5, May 1926, pp. 340–41

Sturm—which was illustrated mainly by the artists he represented, punctuated by critical writing. Late in his life, Gutmann still recalled the pleasure of spending afternoons with a friend, perusing such magazines as *Der Querschnitt* in his favorite cafés. He also contributed sly, satirical drawings to *Die Neue Revue*, a similar publication.

As much as Gutmann enjoyed these sophisticated journals, he was also interested in the more bourgeois weekly illustrated magazines. They were a much more pervasive form of entertainment, published in hundreds of thousands of copies rather than mere hundreds or thousands. These popular magazines were the result of several different technological and social developments in Germany. Newly liberated from censorship, the country evinced an enormous curiosity about the world at large during the Weimar Republic. Most major cities had newspapers that on Sundays produced a special pictorial section illustrated in rotogravure, as many newspapers still produce a weekly magazine today. At the same time, high-speed presses and improved technology made high-quality rotogravure reproductions possible in large quantities on cheap paper, also produced in quantity after the War. These magazines were directed to a large, newly literate audience. Designed to inform as well as entertain, they were enormously successful. Berlin, Hamburg, Cologne, Frankfurt, and Munich all produced important illustrated magazines. In most cases they originated from the local newspaper but often they became independent of their original source. There were others, for example the *A.I.Z.* (*Arbeiter Illustrierte Zeitung*, or *Worker's Illustrated Newspaper*), a worker's party illustrated, and its right-wing counterpart, the Nazi *Illustrierter Beobachter*, as well as more specialized magazines. The *Berliner Illustrirte Zeitung* (which deliberately kept the wrong spelling in its name) emanated from the capital city and was the largest and most prestigious.

Since it was owned by the powerful House of Ullstein firm, it had the most money at its disposal. While it was not always the most lively or visually commanding, during its peak of popularity in the 1920s and 1930s Ullstein could sell two million copies of an issue of the *B.I.Z.* when the population of Germany was forty million. Its closest rival was the *Münchner Illustrierte Presse*, which was founded in 1923. When Hitler was elected Chancellor of Germany in 1933, he seized control of all these magazines and sent them everywhere, including to foreign countries. For him they became tools of a powerful but subtle propaganda.[4]

These magazines followed a successful formula, and, rather surprisingly, it was the text rather than the photographs that interested most of the readers. A serialized novel, usually sentimental in nature, was the chief draw. This so-called book was placed in the middle of the journal, and, if illustrated at all, it was embellished by drawings rather than photographs. For example, *The Grand Hotel*, which was later fashioned into a movie of the same name starring Marlene Dietrich, first appeared in the *B.I.Z.*, and its author, Vicki Baum, was a popular staff writer. Another important feature, or "hook," was the joke page with the newly popular crossword puzzle.

Nevertheless, the role of photography in these magazines was the big innovation. Most often, a photograph was placed on the cover, sometimes spilling over its frame or obscuring the title, an acknowledgment of its greater relationship to life rather than art. Inside, the few pages that were devoted to photography appear casual, jumbled together, or sometimes unclear or meager by today's standards. At most, eight pages were given to photographs, which generally illustrated events in the news, and celebrities. About 1926, they began to include picture stories, which mark the beginning of classic photojournalism. These stories reveal the breadth and depth of the editors' interests, and wonderfully illuminate the later use Gutmann would make of this kind of photography. Early photojournalists generally avoided direct political or social commentary, a fascinating comment in itself, considering that Germany during the Weimar period experienced extreme social upheaval. What are now referred to as "human interest" stories about ancient and unfamiliar customs in rural Germany, the daily lives of workers, housewives, or engineers were common. By the late 1920s pictorial narratives by Martin Munkacsi and Walter Bosshard describing strange lands and foreign peoples and their customs were frequently depicted. Bosshard's cover of an Indian wearing a gas mask is a curiosity, but not a sign of racial superiority (fig. 4). After 1933 such topics would acquire a definite racial bias. Erich Solomon made a reputation photographing what had never been seen before: foreign ministers falling asleep at their international conferences, or the interior of a court in session (fig. 5). The wanderlust of the young, gypsies, and nomads were given much attention, perhaps reflecting a larger cultural anxiety. Other subjects were prominent both before and after Hitler's rise to power. Photographs celebrating physical culture and sports were omnipresent during the Weimar years, a premonition of Leni Riefenstahl's *Olympia*, the film on the 1936 Olympics, and Lothar Rübelt's later pictures in *B.I.Z.* (fig. 6). Stories on the United States that featured New York City skyscrapers and its Depression poor, Chicago gangsters, and the West were also plentiful. After 1933, the German romance with aviation was glorified in the pro-Nazi pictures of Willi Ruge (fig. 7), just as the pictures of Bowery bums (fig. 8) or African culture by Harald Lechenperg and others supported Fascist notions of social and racial superiority.

Although the popular illustrated weeklies displayed no great interest in the serious investigation of photography as

4   *Berliner Illustrirte Zeitung*, November 23, 1930, cover: "Orient von heute," photograph by Bosshard for Dephot agency

5   *Berliner Illustrirte Zeitung*, July 15, 1928, p. 1218: "Die ersten Aufnahmen, die während einer Reichstagssitzung im Saal gemacht Wurden," photographs by Erich Salomon

6   *Berliner Illustrirte Zeitung*, 1935, no. 20, p. 748: "Silhouetten im Blau," photographs by Lothar Rübelt

7 *Berliner Illustrirte Zeitung*, May 15, 1932, pp. 596–97: "Fieseler's 'Tiger II'," photographs by Willi Ruge

8 *Berliner Illustrirte Zeitung*, March 12, 1936, pp. 360–61: "Elend hinter Wolken kratzen," photographs by Harald Lechenper

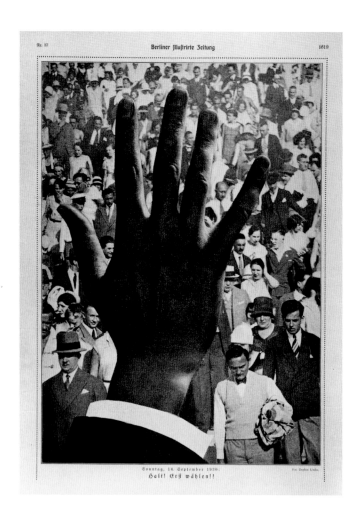

9   *Berliner Illustrirte Zeitung*, September 14, 1930, p. 1619:
    "Halt! Erst Wählem!!" photograph by Umbo for Dephot agency

practised by students and teachers at the Bauhaus, where so-called "New Photography" flourished, when such photography was newsworthy, they reported on it. Occasionally, some Bauhaus-educated photographers, such as Umbo (Otto Umbehr), created vivid collages for a magazine that revealed a high level of sophistication (fig. 9). Other attempts to use photography as a serious artistic vehicle also received attention. When Albert Renger-Patzsch published his modest book *Die Welt ist Schön* (*The World is Beautiful*), around 1928, Thomas Mann's well-illustrated critique appeared in the *B.I.Z.*[5] On the other hand, the art world freely appropriated pictures that appeared in the popular press. When Moholy-Nagy and others at the Bauhaus selected, organized, and published photography in the influential *Film und Foto* exhibition at Stuttgart in 1929,[6] they decontextualized these photographs from the popular magazines. Such popular imagery was also included in the publication *Foto-Auge*, the catalogue with text by Franz Roh, which served as a visual extension of the *Film und Foto* show, as well as a host of other related publications and exhibitions. X-rays, astronomical pictures, anonymous snapshots, as well as commercial and journalistic photography were appropriated with the same avaricious enthusiasm as the work of serious artist photographers. Just as the modern technology of skyscrapers, airplanes, the fad of physical culture, and powerful advertising images appeared in the pages of the *B.I.Z.*, so pictures of these contemporary obsessions were also assimilated by artists.

Innovative popular publications such as the *B.I.Z.* and the *Münchner Illustrierte Presse* especially, along with similar periodicals that later appeared in France and England, inspired the equally rapid growth of American magazines illustrated with photographs, most notably *Life Magazine*, which began publication in 1936. German inventors also changed the way we perceive the world by the instrument made to capture it. Germany produced early hand-held cameras right after World War I—in fact, the most famous and influential, the Leica, had originally been designed before the War to test movie film and went into production soon after the War was over. Unlike elsewhere, particularly the United States, photographers and editors welcomed the Leica in Germany, and many of the photographs in these popular magazines were made with it, or inspired by its spontaneity, its vivid sense of real participation in the stream of life. In addition, these magazines looked very different from the highly sophisticated graphic design promoted by teachers at the Bauhaus. The layouts are playful, too, often deliberately funny or witty, and designed like old-fashioned scrapbooks rather than the now-classic rectangular formats that imitate the camera's predominant vision. Although news photography played an increasingly important role in popular journalism, it was only part of the mix. The *B.I.Z.* and magazines like it were more spontaneous than studied, and, as entertainment, the photographic pages in *B.I.Z.* were relatively free-form and energetic, symptomatic of the beginning of a new enthusiasm rather than a mature formula. Reflecting on his magazine in pre-Fascist Germany, Herman Ullstein remarked that the manager of *B.I.Z.* was a "painter-editor."[7] This is hardly how a corporate magazine such as *Life* would write the job description of one of its major managers.

Gutmann was in his formative years when the picture magazines evolved in Germany, and when he arrived in Berlin the *B.I.Z.* was just entering its most energetic period, a moment when public curiosity and the energy and amused invention of those who worked at the pictorial magazine cohered. Because of Germany's disastrous post-war inflation, many middle-class students originally destined to enter more conventional professions found themselves working for the magazines instead. This was true of Erich Salomon, who had studied law. Art students from the Bauhaus, such as Umbo, found photography a relatively safe way to support themselves, as did Alfred Eisenstadt, who had started as a button salesman, intending to be a businessman.

Such energetic, ambitious photographers and journalists made these magazines more visually engaging and often more compelling than they would later become with professional photojournalists. Who can know whether Lorelle's double-exposure of Brigitte Helm (fig. 10) owed its playful creativity to the unpretentious magazine that published it or to the sophisticated work produced by Bauhaus graduates? Later, as the political landscape changed in Germany, many refugees from Eastern Europe also picked up cameras as a way to keep afloat in a foreign country. Until it fell, France harbored many, as did England. But most of them, including Gutmann, crossed the Atlantic to America.

III   The Transition To America

As a Jew, Gutmann was systematically hamstrung by the Nazis, who virtually prevented him from practising art. In 1933 he was forbidden to exhibit and teach, even though he had full academic qualifications. He saw that he needed to leave and knew that making photographs for magazines would be a useful tool with which to support himself. Gutmann was never trained as a photographer and, in fact, had no interest in the medium as an art form. He had seen none of the now-famous photography exhibitions organized by Bauhaus teachers and their followers, starting with *Film und Foto*. But he was fascinated by and schooled himself in the popular culture of photography in magazines. A month before he sailed for California, Gutmann purchased a Rolleiflex—a new camera that had appeared on the market

10   *Berliner Illustrirte Zeitung*, January 13, 1929, cover:
   "Brigitte Helm," photograph by Lorelle

the previous year—read the instructions, made three rolls of test shots that are precursors of his later work, and obtained a contract with an agency, Presse-Foto, to send pictures back to Germany for the magazines.

Unlike most of Germany's refugees entering the United States, Gutmann did not stop in New York but went directly to San Francisco. A friend of his, the editor of *Die Neue Revue* who had published some of his clever drawings, had advised him to leave Europe altogether. Gerhard von Godhart, whose rich mother was an American, told his friend, "There is only one country, that is the United States, the only state is California, the only city, San Francisco."[8] The major port city of the West Coast, San Francisco, was a wide-open town in the 1930s, still possessing the edgy spirit it earned during the gold rush. New York, as he was later to discover, was home to many European immigrants, and would harbor more in a very short time, but no other European artist of his background emigrated to San Francisco. While it was common in the East to look toward Europe, in the West attention was more commonly directed to Asia, a place as alluring as it was remote to him. Of all Western cities, San Francisco has been ethnically and culturally diverse since even before its Mexican history, another factor that he found deeply compelling as a recent racial outcast. In the 1930s, without the presence of television or fast airplanes, it seemed more remote and more exotic than today, especially for someone coming from Nazi Germany. It also possessed a mild, temperate climate. For the visitor Gutmann, the city proved richly evocative and highly stimulating. He said, "I was in Paradise."[9]

Gutmann soon installed himself among the expatriate intellectual community. One of his earliest and best friends was Walter Heil, the Director of the M.H. de Young Museum, who had arrived in about 1926. Another was Siegfried Aram, who had been a judge in Germany and supported his taste for partying and women by gradually selling the Old Master paintings he arranged to remove from his castle back home. Gutmann had little knowledge and less interest in those photographers in the Bay Area who were conscientiously converting the photographic medium into an aesthetic tool—photographers such as Edward Weston, Ansel Adams, and Imogen Cunningham of the f/64 group. These artists had just been given their famous show at the de Young Museum in 1932, and their subjects, their connoisseur's approach toward the print, and, for most of them, the spiritual content of their art were diametrically opposed to Gutmann's interests. An informed city-dweller, one who found delight among the curiosities and diversities afforded by such a town as San Francisco, Gutmann was never interested in the unpeopled or conventionally beautiful landscape. More importantly, he never presumed that in making photographs he was producing art. He considered the two enterprises entirely separate. Late in his life Gutmann observed that he knew only slightly what was happening in California's rural agricultural areas, in places visited and documented by Dorothea Lange and others. Instead, shortly after his arrival, Gutmann focused his camera on the strangeness, the oddities of this new urban environment, to which he, as a foreign visitor, was particularly sensitive. Though he took a Greyhound bus up the coast to Canada soon after his arrival, his metropolitan vision remained intact, focused, and genuinely close in spirit to the wit, voyeurism, and impatient curiosity of the magazine culture he had recently left. There was an important difference, however: in the German magazines every subject was considered with interest. Statesmen, as well as the small circus performers in rural Germany, were made equally curious, or funny, or remarkable (fig. 11).

The common man or ordinary citizen was as frequently photographed (if not more so) than politicians, movie stars, and aristocrats. When Salomon photographed the events in

a stock exchange for the first time, it was to discover how human and almost predictable the proceedings really were (fig. 12). To Gutmann's eye, on the other hand, everything in America was exotic or strange.

Gutmann's work in these early years has a Surrealist cast, a quality of psychic instability that differentiates his pictures from those of most of his German contemporaries. Gutmann did not indulge in satire, however; in fact, he refrained from judgment, he only observed. He had a taste for the morbid, the darkly sexual, the strange that was neither an element of German magazine populism nor even, for the most part, of German art photography— which, if anything, was usually utopian in spirit. Part of this strangeness can be attributed to his chosen tool of representation, a 2¼ x 2¼ twin-lens reflex Rolleiflex camera held at the waist, which changed the described space by its unusual angle of vision. This format was distinct from that of the German magazine photographers, who commonly used a 35 mm viewfinder camera such as the Leica (or its slower relative, the Erminox), and from the f/64 photographers, who usually employed the view camera to produce their meditative and highly detailed images. The Rolleiflex distorted Gutmann's subjects and placed them in a disorienting space. His pictures possess a compelling psychological quality, accentuated by their sharp shadows and strong diagonal forms. They also convey a sense of remoteness or distance akin to the point of view of an anthropologist examining an exotic culture.[10]

By 1934 Gutmann had examined the California coast from San Francisco to Vancouver, and two years later he took an extended Greyhound bus tour around the United States. He spent four months in New York, but, just as important, he traveled south, to New Orleans, Georgia, and Alabama, to the Midwest, and the Southwest. He changed his affiliation from Presse-Foto to one with the more established

11 *Berliner Illustrirte Zeitung*, November 6, 1927, p. 1835:
"Sensation im Dorf: Der Wanderzirkus Kommt!"
photographs by A. and E. Franke

12 *Berliner Illustrirte Zeitung*, September 14, 1930, pp. 1660–61

13   *Der Ring Illustrierte*, 1934: "Eine Photoreportage vom
      Generalstreik in San Francisco," from John Gutmann's scrapbook

igene Börse und Kirche im Haus," photographs by Erich Salomon

Frog Jumpers' Grand National

IN the rough and tumble days of the gold rushes, Angels' Camp, in California, was a booming town of gold miners. These miners were born gamblers. Besides on cards and dice, they laid wagers on jumping frogs, which they bred. This town and its jumping frogs were immortalised by Mark Twain in his story, "The Jumping Frog of Calaveras." He tells how two smart New York confidence men came to the camp, backed an ordinary garden frog against the town champion. The owner of the champion jumper rushed out to catch a "commoner," leaving his precious frog with the New Yorkers, who, during his absence, filled the animal with buckshot . . . A large crowd saw the town champion beaten by a common frog! When the fraud was discovered, the two impostors had long since disappeared. In honor of this famous event, Angels' Camp has, for the last twelve years, staged a jumping jubilee, reviving the Gold Rush days.

Ready For The Big Jump. Entries for the championship included frogs from Puerto Rico, Switzerland and all over America. Frogs jump from a white circle on ground.

One Of The Frogs entered in the International championship at Angels' Camp. Here he is seen after the second of the three jumps allowed him.

Authentic Period Costumes are worn by residents for the two days of the frog jumping jubilee. Here frog stickers and badges are distributed by one of the committee.

SEPTEMBER 23, 1939.   P I X——Page Thirty

14   *Pix*, September 23, 1939, p. 30: "Frog Jumpers' Grand National,"
     from John Gutmann's scrapbook

agency Pix (which was also more conveniently located in New York), and many of the pictures he made on these excursions were published not only in the United States, but also in Europe, where they were wholly within the tradition of the German bourgeois magazines. Residing now in the West, Gutmann submitted picture stories of local oddities: the chicken industry in the northern California town of Petaluma (pls. 24, 25), where there was even a chicken pharmacy; the opening of the 1939 World's Fair in San Francisco (pl. 79); the activities of the large Asian population in the city, and, for the *B.I.Z.*, the San Francisco waterfront strike of 1934 (fig. 13, pl. 68), which stirred ominous reverberations for the photographer. From his travels, Gutmann sold pictures of an African-American convent in New Orleans and of New York City's Harlem (pl. 12). Many individual pictures were later extracted from these pictorial essays, such as the mysterious photograph of a pointing hand, a portentous shadow and a disembodied white circle on the ground called *The Jump* (pl. 96), which had been made as part of a story on the famous frog-jumping contest Mark Twain described, an event that still takes place in Calaveras County (fig. 14). Making these pictures for his journalistic clients in these places also enabled Gutmann to make pictures for himself. The posture of tourist or visitor enabled him to see otherwise commonplace or amusing subjects with awe.

Gutmann published photographs regularly, especially in the early years. His work frequently appeared in *Coronet*, a pocket-sized magazine edited in Chicago by an immigrant Hungarian named Arnold Gingrich (fig. 15). This magazine was a populist version of *Der Querschnitt*. Pictures in *Coronet* were selected by someone familiar with the aesthetic of European modernist photography, and were published either singly or in amusing or poignant pairings. Many émigré photographers, such as André Kertesz and Alfred

15   *Coronet*, July 1939, pp. 82–83 (Gutmann's picture, *Class* [pl. 39], on right)

16 *Life Magazine*, March 6, 1939: "The Pageant of the Pacific," from John Gutmann's scrapbook

Eisenstadt, saw their work accepted in its pages, and it was one of the few places that featured and discussed contemporary European photography. Besides publishing single pictures, *Coronet* often printed an extensive profile on a recognized photographer. In this way *Coronet* published work by Henri Cartier-Bresson and Brassaï, for example, as well as by Americans such as Berenice Abbott. Gutmann's work also appeared in the Edward Steichen and T.J. Maloney annual compendium of photographs, *US Camera*. This was the only other magazine in the United States that treated individual pictures with attention and dignity. Its editors celebrated the aesthetic potential of pictures in the commercial and journalistic fields and mixed them with self-consciously artistic photographs, not always successfully. All different approaches were treated equally.

As was not uncommon in the early years of photojournalism, Gutmann's stories were published in newspapers as well as in popular magazines such as *Look* and *The Saturday Evening Post*. His photographs of the 1939 World's Fair (fig. 16) and the unveiling of a monument to Sun Yat-Sen in San Francisco's Chinatown appeared in *Life*. The *Detroit News Pictorial* published his account of the efforts by the Chinese community in San Francisco to raise money to fight the Japanese, a story that reflected contemporary concerns as well as his personal interests. Accompanied by the photographer's own texts, Gutmann's picture stories also appeared in German pictorial magazines, including the venerable *Berliner Illustrirte Zeitung*. German papers ran the émigré's essays on training American soldiers, on San Francisco's Chinese residents and their culture, on his adopted city's precipitous streets and the cable-cars designed to climb them, on the curious customs aboard a ship crossing the equator (this was documented during Gutmann's trip to San Francisco), on western rodeos (pl. 41), and the black women's school in Atlanta, Spelman College.

Following his full-time appointment as Professor of Art at San Francisco State College in 1938, Gutmann's magazine work became sporadic. During the war years, 1942–45, he studied at the Signal Corps Motion Picture School in Astoria, Queens, and made both still and motion pictures for the US Army Signal Corps. During the War, too, and in its wake, Gutmann focused his attention on China and published on this and other Asian cultures (fig. 17, pls. 91–95). Stories of these places appeared in *National Geographic, Asia, Geographic Magazine*, and other periodicals.

IV Gutmann's Art

Making pictures to sell was not Gutmann's only incentive to carry his camera around with him. The making of pictures became a means to analyze the new culture he experienced, one more deeply populist and materialistic than the one he had been obliged to abandon. In almost stereotypical Germanic fashion, he proceeded to categorize the aspects of American culture he wanted to document, and these divisions—"Documents of the Street" and "The Automobile," for example—remain evident in his exhibitions and publications. He discovered that, unlike their German counterparts, American artists were not generally attracted to such analytic examination. Gutmann was somewhat irritated by the "spiritual" content in California art, not only in the rather provincial painting he found when he arrived, but also in the seriousness and self-consciousness of photographers such as Adams and Weston. He generally excluded himself from the company of artists and became instead a dedicated, but removed, connoisseur of American low-life and popular culture.

Some of the photographs made in the 1930s appear almost to be a conscious analysis of American life directly related to the approach of the German magazines. Thus, Gutmann's pictures of divers and gymnasts must relate, even subconsciously, to the great German interest in physical culture that became in Fascist Germany (and simultaneously in the Soviet Union) a symbol of self-reliance, of freedom, and of emerging power. Gutmann's pictures *The Swimmer, Class: Olympic High Diving Champion, Marjorie Gestrinz*, and *Out of the Pool, San Francisco* (pls. 37, 39, 44) are more resonant when compared with Alexander Rodchenko's early constructivist picture *Diver* (1935), to Lothar Rübelt's pictures of divers and other athletes, and to Leni Riefenstahl's pictures and her propagandistic film *Olympia* on the 1936 Olympic Games.[11] Other photographs, notably those depicting African-American life, especially in the South, or the photograph of the Chinese playground (pl. 81) and those responding to the Japanese presence in San Francisco, would have had particular reverberations to one accustomed to the exclusionary racial policies of Fascist Germany. The photographs Gutmann made of war preparedness, such as *Before Pearl Harbor, ROTC at Mission High School, San Francisco* (pl. 78), or the general strike, and especially the picture he called *Omen* (pl. 2), which recorded three airplanes aloft in a blank San Francisco sky, were the uninflected, unheroic, even ironic and fearful antitheses of pictures glorifying the might and unity of the German army and the heroism of the Luftwaffe.

There were two other major subjects Gutmann pursued with a fascination bordering on obsession: the American passion for the automobile and America's prurient fascination with sex. In Germany, cars were not the objects of lavish attention, nor were they as commonplace as in the United States. Gutmann said that when he arrived in America, he was surprised to see so many of them during the Depression, and he vividly recalled his astonishment at seeing people drive their cars to the relief offices. In Europe,

17 *Panorama*, 37, no. 20, May 19, 1950: "Pelgrimage der Chinezen," from John Gutmann's scrapbook

the automobile was the possession of the wealthy, and their cars were as luxurious as they were rare. When he was a child, Gutmann's family had a car and chauffeur, and he remembered his sense of privilege driving in it. In fact, there were no gas stations in Germany, since the chauffeurs also maintained the cars. In America, it was Henry Ford's aim for every American who wanted a car to have one. Gutmann learned to drive and owned a car only after he married at the end of the War.

It is fascinating to realize that German photographers of the inter-war period rarely depicted cars or the car culture, probably because of their relative scarcity. German and Russian photography, however, both reveal a deep and prevalent fascination, even a romance, with the machine. The most intellectual artist to be smitten with the romantic mythology of the machine was probably Moholy-Nagy, who used machine parts to construct his photograms, converting the objects into tools of ideal abstraction. His "telephone paintings" were so called because he made them out of absolute geometric shapes of contemporary machined materials and instructed a fabricator, over the telephone, to assemble them. Constructivist art idealized the engineer, the builder of bridges, radio towers, and the new architecture. When cars appear in these pictures they are part of a land-scape seen from above, part of the larger fabric of modern life. In both Russia and Germany, the ideal of the machine-like image, or the machine itself, was utopian, a symbolic turning away from old systems, political as well as artistic ones. The machine was a symbol of a new, rational, and democratic order, usually dominated by man's intelligence. Perhaps the most potent image of this is El Lissitzky's famous picture The Constructor (1924), used for the cover of the catalogue of Franz Roh's Foto-Auge.[12] Hand and head are conjoined at the architect-artist's eye, the hand holding a compass from which emanate a grid and stenciled letters,

forming a kind of elliptical halo around the portrait head. The human eye and mind control the ideal plan, the new mechanical order.

Gutmann never felt comfortable with ideals, and his photographic work concentrated on the particular. American art photography, which preceded and influenced European modernist photography, also demonstrated more of an affinity for the particular than the ideal, even with its idealist inflection. Paul Strand and Ralph Steiner, for example, made close-up abstractions of automobiles, and many other Americans also photographed this subject. While their pictures idealize this machine, abstracting the subject to conform to modernist artistic principles, they are also photographs of particular cars, usually the very car belonging to the photographer who took their picture. Whereas in Europe the photograph, made by a machine, the camera, was situated within the symbolism of the utopian vision of the new engineer, in the United States photographers perceived their challenge as eliciting a kind of modern art from a recalcitrant mechanical medium, one that would honor both art and its own inherent properties: detail, sharpness, the close-up, etc.[13] Gutmann's work, essentially documentary, was different from both these approaches.

Gutmann began to photograph Americans with their automobiles almost as soon as he arrived in the United States in 1934. One of his first responses was to the prevalence of automobiles: in cities and the countryside, they were driven by everyone, rich as well as poor. Gutmann marveled that people without homes drove around the great open spaces of the West, looking for work in the large corporate plantations in California, escaping their small, dried-up farms in Oklahoma, Texas, and Arkansas, bringing their possessions with them, tied to the roofs and sides of their cars (pl. 10). In 1936, Gutmann saw a man who had converted his broken-down, tireless car into an office.

On its windshield, someone had written, "Pay as you enter" (*The Office*, 1936). Chinese laundrymen delivered their hand-washed shirts in their cars (*Chinese Laundry, San Francisco*, 1934) and a new ignition system was publicly demonstrated on the hood of another (*The New Gadget, San Francisco*, 1935). People slept in their cars on the street (pl. 60) and they also ate in their cars (pls. 22, 23). We know they made love in their cars, but in 1935 they also went to the movies in them (pls. 20, 21). One of his early pictures from Berlin, taken just before he left in 1933 (*Autumn in Charlottenberg, Berlin*, 1933), shows a busy sidewalk, a Nazi flag, and a single car in the street. On the first day he arrived in 1934, he recalled that the streets of the United States were cluttered with cars. High-school students drove to public school and parked on the facing street (*Students' Cars Parked at Galileo High School, San Francisco*, 1934) and bathers took their cars to the beach (*Automobiles Parked at a Beach, Oregon*, 1934). Everyone, it seemed, ironically, took their car to the park, presumably to enjoy a moment with-out cars (*Parking in the Park, San Francisco*, 1935). Strange structures were made to transport cars (*Automobile Transport, Chicago*, 1936) or to house them temporarily (pls. 5, 6). In Harlem, the car was treated with special iconic reverence (pl. 12) and the sign he saw in Detroit, reading "Switch to Dodge," he called *An American Altar* (pl. 16). Cars were decorated with stylized flying women (pl. 11), flying dragons (*The Dragon, San Francisco*, 1938), bears, flying horses, sexy women, and a sign reading "God is Love." In 1938, during one of the most divisive elections in California, when the so-called "Ham and Eggs" petition proposed giving thirty dollars per week to those past fifty, a car pulled up to the Mission Produce Co., covered with hand-painted messages (pl. 74). "Yes, Columbus did discover America," it read, "We have discovered the international bankers have taken it away from us saps!" To a recent Jewish immigrant, painfully

familiar with such abusive rhetoric, this must have been as unsettling as it was fascinating. Gutmann's attention to cars, part of the romance of modernism, is really its opposite: evidence not of the ideal but the touchingly and tragically human, indications of an American love of individualism at once funny and isolating.

V Themes of Love and Death

Gutmann's admiration for the circus, especially the highwire aerialist's act and the trick riding of the bareback dancer, as well as his fondness for making pictures of physical culture, gymnastics, and skilled diving all had precedents in popular representations in Germany. His numerous pictures of people poised in the air, falling, or jumping perilously over a horse's hindquarters (pls. 36, 38, 41) also suggest his fascination with a state of freedom and loss of control, of potential regeneration and annihilation. These states are commonly associated with the act of sex and the moment of death.

Themes of love and death, central to the human experience, have also been central in art. Pablo Picasso can be said to have claimed these as his key and constant pre-occupations. Both *Guernica* (1937) and *Tauromachia* (1957–59) conjoin gored bulls with beautiful, bare-breasted women. The pairing of seeming opposites was also explored by the Surrealists, who were also fascinated by these two subjects and committed to the investigation of their inter-relationship.[14] To varying degrees, these themes occupy a large portion of Gutmann's work.

The consciousness of death was always important in Germanic art, an example being *The Dance of Death* (1538) by Hans Holbein the Younger, which Gutmann admired. The subject also preoccupied Edvard Munch (1863–1944), another Northern artist whom Gutmann admired throughout his life. Shortly after his arrival in San Francisco, Gutmann started to collect death objects and images, inspired, perhaps, by the large Hispanic population, which celebrates death more openly (and erotically) than in his own culture. He was making these discoveries at the same time, and with the same intensity, as he was exploring the erotic diversity of the city.[15]

Soon after settling in California, Gutmann noticed a strange figure, gloved, wrapped in a gauzy veil that covered her from her hat to her carefully stockinged feet. Her obscured face appeared to him to resemble a death-mask. He marveled that one so peculiarly dressed went unmolested: in Germany, he knew, she would be taunted, and compelled to change, but in this country, odd as she appeared, she was free. He called the picture *Death Stalks Fillmore* (pl. 50). The same year, he photographed a beautiful young woman dressed in black, her coat trimmed with fur, her black curls carefully lacquered, whom he had observed seated on a rampart overlooking the waterfront and looming large, neither coquettish nor proud, but very present. She appeared to him like a vision or some powerful ancient force dominating the young sailors, her silhouette carved from the cold light. He called this dark, strange picture *The Fleet Is In, San Francisco* (pl. 46).[16]

Women have been a central interest to Gutmann throughout his life. His attitude toward them was like that of the Surrealists: to him, they represented a strong, magical force, inarticulate, irresistible, sometimes enticingly dangerous. Looking at Gutmann's work is often like being reminded of André Breton's novel *Nadja* (1928). Usually in Gutmann's pictures, women are not seen intimately or even personally, but they possess a mystery, a charm or allure of their sex. Each is not a woman, singular, but "woman."

Gutmann photographed women from the vantage-point of voyeurism. "*Alice from Dallas, World's Fattest Girl,*"

San Francisco (pl. 89) sits above the viewer on a stage: large, horrible, but with an uncanny, real power, frightening and vital, a mysterious light glowing around her spread legs. She is seen from the same point of view as the more alluring woman, dressed in a shiny bathing-suit, her belly and pudendum bulging in *Day Dreams* (1939), and *Bare Back, San Francisco* (pl. 41), a picture of the trick-rider's wide-kicking leg upon the horse's own flank, its vein twitching prominently. In pictures taken around the swimming-pool, Gutmann eliminates the head, or chops off unnecessary limbs, focusing his attention on the torso (pl. 37). The same could be said of the photographs he made of Count Basie at the San Francisco World's Fair of 1939—pictures of unalloyed joy and admiration for what he saw as the sexual energy of these black American entertainers, seen from the point of view of a spectator (pls. 82, 83). Like many Europeans, including, for instance, Robert Frank, Gutmann romanticized not only the freedom African-Americans gained from their isolation in American society, but also their sexual joy.

Gutmann recognized the opposing allures of sex and death commingled in New Orleans at the Mardi Gras festivities in 1937. Germany has its own anti-hierarchical and anti-authoritarian carnival celebration, *Faschung*, when rigid class divisions are dissolved and anarchy briefly rules. Much more interesting to this German photographer was transgressing racial boundaries in New Orleans. As was also true in Germany, most participants wore masks to prevent discovery of their true identity. But in Gutmann's pictures, the white masks on black women, or the white-masked women in dark, masculine riding outfits (pl. 56) are both alluring and frightening. The woman who spreads her arms in *Jitterbug, New Orleans* (pl. 58) flutters almost angelic wings and wears a deathly-white mask. So does the taunting, screaming partner of *In the Background: The Pimp,*

New Orleans (pl. 59). The dangerous attractions of love, or the pairing of pleasure and torture, appeared in one of his grimmest pictures, *Sex and Crime* (pl. 33), of a San Francisco storefront he discovered where pin-ups, a demonstration of Chinese torture, and the FBI hunting for gangsters meet in sinister proximity.

Gutmann has always had an affinity for the pairing of opposites, and has aspired to make art that provokes questions, or leaves the viewer unsettled. His work is replete with apparent contradictions or evocative pairings, much in the manner of Surrealism. He has also been interested in sexual deviance, just as he has been in racial transgression. Pairs appear frequently in his photographs, sometimes lesbian couples—for example, *Two Women in Love* (1937) and *Shrug of the Shoulder* (pl. 45)—or emotionally troubled couples, as in *Portrait of a Marriage* (pl. 47).[17]

After Gutmann began to teach at San Francisco State University in 1938, he had less time to pursue street photography as freely as when he first arrived in the country. The themes that preoccupied him earlier recur in photographs he took as a member of the Signal Corps in the entirely exotic cultures in India, China, and Southeast Asia, as in *Dead Hindu Girl Awaiting Burning at the Pyres of the Nimtolla Ghat, Calcutta* and *Advertisement of a Sex Specialist for the Treatment of World Famous Diseases, Calcutta* (both 1945). Many of his Asian pictures are anthropological without the Surrealist mystery that informed the early pictures made in the United States.

After the War, Gutmann returned to the studio. A large three-panel screen produced in 1946–47 constitutes both a summary of his life as an artist, and his re-entry (fig. 18). Poised in the middle, dominating all three sections, is the figure of the artist-photographer, a Rolleiflex near his eye, a flash in his left hand, an easel to his right, and beneath him, brushes and students' paintings. On the reverse,

Gutmann painted the figure of a nude woman. Her body extended to include the three panels, she seems to float or fall in an undifferentiated space. From every angle of Gutmann's body emanate eyes—cut-outs from a fashion magazine—and scattered all over the background are cut-up photographs, dizzying in their number and variety. Faces predominate, many large ones counterbalancing countless small heads, backs, bodies, and bowls of food. The impression is of a voracious observer, feasting on the varieties of visual experience divided equally between his earlier San Francisco pictures and the photographs of Asia he had more recently completed. It is a complex work of art: neither strictly painting nor pure collage, made at a time when he was not acquainted with such Bay Area artists as Bruce Conner and Jess, who would extensively explore the potential of photo collage.

The screen also signals both a renewed investigation of the self-portrait and a turn toward greater manipulation in his photography. Gutmann had made self-portraits before, for example the revealing *Self-Portrait with Love Bird* (pl. 99), in which a blurry portrait of the artist hovers beneath his bolder painting. He also began constructing self-portraits, for instance the double-exposed *Death Trap* (1936), a picture of his opened mouth revealing his portrait, and *Photoplasmic Self-Portrait* (1937), in which he put a glass bubble in his mouth and twine over his face in a dark, collage-like, Surrealist space.

Just months after completing the complicated screen, he photographed a beautiful, sensuous, and extraordinarily photogenic woman seated in front of it, smoking a cigarette. This was Gerry von Pribosic, whom he would marry the next year and photograph frequently. An enormously gifted artist herself, she was also deeply troubled, and would finally take her own life. For Gutmann, Gerry was the very embodiment of sex and death.

18   John Gutmann, *Folding Screen*, 1946–47. Gelatin-silver prints, tempera on panel, three panels, each 72 x 24 in.

San Francisco Museum of Modern Art, photograph by John Gutmann

He photographed her in a variety of poses: veiled; paired with another woman, as in *The Oracle* (pl. 49); or drinking a cup of coffee on their bed, under a picture of him and beside one of her paintings. Mainly, however, he photographed her obsessive attraction to her "Father Doll," a toy she constructed, coddled, and tortured, a memory of the father who had deserted her in childhood (*Father Doll*, 1951). In *Father Doll Watching Lovers on a Swing* (1951), the doll's head is broken, empty, and mask-like, and he hovers over the folk-art lovers like a ghostly specter.

V Conclusion

Gutmann's art is essentially that of a European, fascinated by the culture he found in the New World but isolated from it. He protected this vision by remaining aloof from the people who made art in his adopted city; his close friends and associates tended to be intellectuals from Europe. He also protected his vision by consciously separating painting, which he took very seriously, from photography. After his initial activity documenting the culture of America, he confused the two, and yet insisted on the great difference and special character of each.

John Gutmann's art was anomalous within the culture in which he finally made his home. The work he produced is really the diametric opposite of what Northern California art and photography have come to represent. In painting, Bay Area art is associated with the cool, succulent color, the pleasing abstraction of Richard Diebenkorn and Sam Francis, or the no less sensuous figurative painting of Elmer Bischoff and Nathan Oliveira. The Mediterranean-like climate and remarkable natural beauty of the area have produced a culture that takes pleasure in the out-of-doors, sensuous and austere at once. Most of the homes have expansive windows; they are decorated by light and astonishing views. In such circumstances art can seem superfluous, photography even more so.

Gutmann's own house overlooked the Bay and the Golden Gate Bridge and was located near the Haight-Ashbury neighborhood, the scene of the colorful dissipation of the "flower children" of the 1960s and their successors. It looks down into the city but is aloof from it. The rest of the home was kept characteristically dark, to protect his expansive collection of books, mainly European, and his collection of African and other tribal art. Gutmann created an island of European culture to come home to—a darker vision in a light-drenched city.

Trained as a painter, accredited as a teacher by an inspired and important German Expressionist artist, an acute appreciator of the culture of inter-war Berlin, Gutmann made a unique contribution in his photographs of San Francisco, the city "half a world away" from his cultural origin, but one that he was predisposed to admire by temperament and aesthetic training. By taking up the camera as almost an afterthought, and by insisting that it carry no aesthetic burden, Gutmann freed himself to record all the strangeness and diversity of the bizarre and marvelous culture of the United States that so attracted him. Insulated from outsiders, he was unaffected and unaware of the great place photography enjoyed in Northern California as an expressive form of art in its own right. His initial excited vision was modified over time: he used the camera during his military service in the Far East, producing pictures of an almost anthropological nature, without the surreal magic of his depictions of the United States. Later, he experimented with more deliberate, constructed photography, in a manner related to his work as a painter.

Gradually Gutmann's photography diminished, and his painting as well, until he was rediscovered as a photographer in the 1970s. That late work is ingenious and mannered, continuing his interest in the signage of a foreign (and, in this case, electrified) culture. As he continued to live in the city, much of his later effort was devoted to teaching: he became first a part-time instructor at San Francisco State College, then a full-time professor, teaching modern art and art history in a city where there was little knowledge of modern art. This also was a welcome challenge to him. His students were genuinely unaware of the culture he had left,

and he found the responsibility of bringing an understanding of European art to a distant city to be a compelling and engrossing task. Although it may seem fragmented, Gutmann's professional career is consistent with his interests. As an outsider, a Jew in his original culture, he needed to understand culture as a human experience, one that he observed, photographed, painted, collected, or imparted on individual terms.

1   Published originally as *The Last of Mr Norris* (1935) and as *Mr Norris Changes Trains* (1937), the collection received its now-familiar title in the 1945 edition.

2   Gutmann says that the figure of the bellboy to the right in *Chocolate Kiddies*—who is not an African-American—was influenced by his familiarity with Oskar Schlemmer's work.

3   *Der Querschnitt* initiated the amusing pairing of unrelated pictures, which, transformed, survive in *Spy* magazine's "Separated at Birth" pictures.

4   Most copies of these magazines available in the United States are those sent to public libraries after Hitler assumed power. The earlier (and more numerous) examples are now extremely rare.

5   December 28, 1928.

6   The *Film und Foto* exhibition inaugurated a whole series of photographic shows, mainly in Germany, featuring the "New Photography" but including appropriated pictures as well.

7   Herman Ullstein, *The Rise and Fall of the House of Ullstein*, New York (Simon & Schuster) 1943, p. 79. Ullstein is describing Kurt Safranski, who, as a member of the board, occupied a position "not unlike that of a film producer." For further information on the early years of German photojournalism see Tim N. Gidal, *Modern Photojournalism: Origin and Evolution, 1910–33*, New York (Collier Books) 1973, and Ute Eskildsen, "Fotografie in deutschen Zeitschriften, 1924–1933," in *Eine Austellung des Institute fur Auslandsbeziehungen*, Stuttgart 1982.

8   Cited by Marvin Heiferman in *John Gutmann: 99 Fotografías, America, 1934–1954*, Barcelona (Fundació Caixa de Pensions) 1989, p. 8.

9   Statements by John Gutmann are based on a series of interviews conducted by the author.

10 Gutmann said he was somewhat aware of Surrealist art when he lived in Germany, but was never terribly interested in it.

11 At this same time Moholy-Nagy also included a high-diver in his photocollage *Leda and the Swan*, which was more of a personal than a political statement.

12 Franz Roh and Jan Tschichold (eds.), *Photo-eye: 76 Photos of the Period* [*ca.* 1929], New York (Arno Press) 1973. This volume was produced in tandem with the *Film und Foto* exhibition at Stuttgart.

13 See Christopher Phillips, "Resurrecting Vision: The New Photography in Europe Between the Wars," in *The New Vision: Photography Between the World Wars. Ford Motor Company Collectors at the Metropolitan Museum of Art*, ed. Maria Hambourg and Christopher Phillips, New York (Abrams) 1989, pp. 65–108.

14 See *L'Amour Fou: Photography and Surrealism*, exhib. cat. by Rosalind Krauss *et al.*, Washington, D.C., Corcoran Gallery of Art, 1985.

15 Until his death, Gutmann always wore a skull on his lapel as a form of talisman against death.

16 Gutmann did not know if she was a prostitute or not, but deeply associated her with sex. He said she knew "she could get good sex from sailors away from land for months."

17 *Portrait of a Marriage* owes its energy to the fact that the husband was gay, a fact Gutmann learned after the man's death.

The Photographs

The photographs are all gelatin-silver prints measuring either 11 x 14 or 14 x 11 inches
except pls. 1, 21, 22, 25, 28, 66, 67, 68, 75, and 79, which measure either 8 x 10 or 10 x 8 inches.

1 | *Self-Portrait, San Francisco* 1934

2 | *Omen* 1934

3 | *The Open Window* 1939

4 | *American Landscape V, Chicago* 1939

5 | *Elevator Garage, Chicago* 1936

6 | *Elevator Garage with Parking Lot* 1936

7 | *From the North Tower of Golden Gate Bridge, San Francisco* 1947

8 | *Maintenance Worker Moving Down Main Cable of Golden Gate Bridge, San Francisco* 1947

9 | *Cash for Your Car, San Francisco* 1939

10 | *Okies on Their Way West, Laramie, Wyoming* 1935

11 | *Reach, San Francisco* 1938

12 | *Cord in Harlem, New York City* 1936

13 | *Bicycle of a Mexican Barber, San Antonio* 1937

14 | *Wyoming Car* 1936

15 | *Nob Hill, San Francisco* 1938

16 | *"Switch to Dodge," An American Altar, Detroit* 1936

17 | *"Time Flies … Save Now!"* 1947

18 | *Barber School, Bowery, New York City* 1936

19 | *Pop Advertising, San Francisco* 1939

20 | *First Drive-In Theater, Los Angeles* 1935

21 | *Inside the First Drive-In Theater in Los Angeles* 1935

22 | *Early Drive-In Restaurant, Los Angeles* 1935

23 | *"Eat in Car," Early Drive-In Restaurant, Hollywood* 1935

24 | *Monument to the Chicken Center of the World, Petaluma, California* 1936

25 | *"The World's Egg Basket," Petaluma, California* 1938

26 | *The Artist Lives Dangerously, San Francisco* 1938

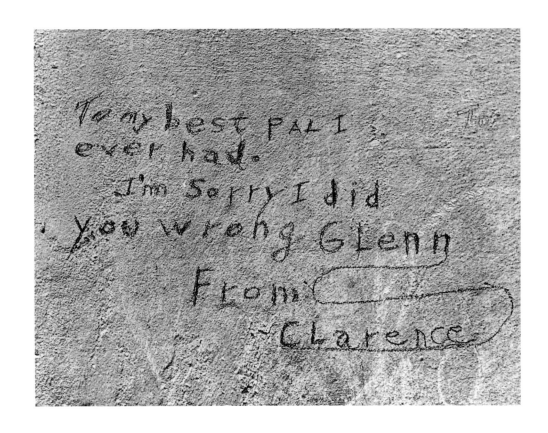

27 | *Apology, San Francisco* 1938

28 | *"Lost What," San Francisco* 1938

29 | *"Baron Von Hoffman for President"* 1939

31 | *Sign (Seeds) California* 1937

32 | *Ben's Barbershop Window: "Streamlined Hair Cut"* 1946

33 | *Sex and Crime* 1935

34 | *Girlie Mags, San Francisco* 1937

35 | *"Man's Ruin" Tattoo* 1945

36 | *Spotting the Somersaults* 1939

37 | *The Swimmer* 1934

38 | *The Fall* 1934

39 | *Class: Olympic High Diving Champion, Marjorie Gestrinz* 1936

40 | *Majorette* 1939

41 | *Bare Back, San Francisco* 1939

42 | *Voyeur, Alarmed* 1938

43 | *Drill Team of Puerto Rican Cowgirls Waiting for 5th Avenue Parade* 1979

44 | *Out of the Pool, San Francisco* 1934

45 | *Shrug of the Shoulder* 1935

46 | *The Fleet Is In, San Francisco* 1934

47 | *Portrait of a Marriage* 1935

48 | *Turning to Look* 1935

50 | *Death Stalks Fillmore* 1934

51 | *Memory* 1939

52 | *Texas Women* 1937

53 | *The Lesson, Central Park, New York* 1936

54 | *Cynics, Hollywood* 1934

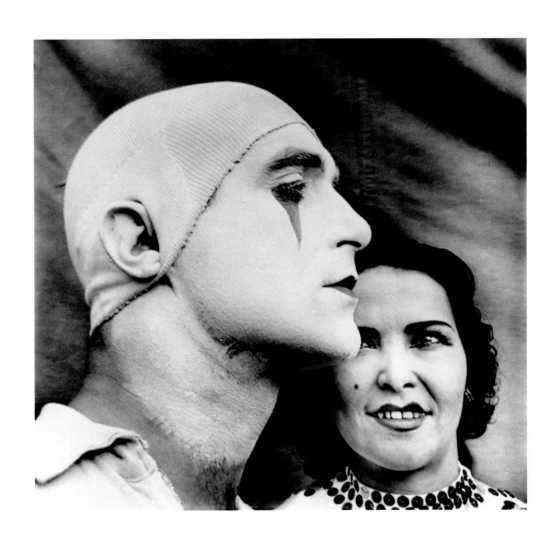

55 | *The Beautiful Clown* 1940

56 | *The Game, New Orleans* 1937

57 | *October, Berlin* 1933

58 | *Jitterbug, New Orleans* 1937

59 | *In the Background: The Pimp, New Orleans* 1937

60 | *Dream of Uprising* 1935

61 | *The Killer* 1948

62 | *Mobile, Alabama* 1937

63 | *"We're Not Talking," Lovelock, Nevada* 1936

64 | *Blackjack in Reno at Election Time, Nevada* 1936

65 | "*W.P.A.*," *San Francisco* 1937

66 | *Avant Guard* 1939

67 | *Pickets, Maritime Strike, New York* 1936

68 | *"We Want the 40 Hour Week," San Francisco* 1934

69 | *The Orator* 1939

70 | *"Ham and Eggs," San Francisco* 1938

71 | *Raging Madness—Young Secrets* 1957

72 | *Anti-Fascist Posters, San Francisco* 1938

73 | *The News Photographer, San Francisco City Hall* 1935

74 | *"Yes, Columbus Did Discover America," San Francisco* 1938

75 | *Che Guevara, Malcolm X, Rosa Luxemburg, et al. at the "Militant Forum" Bookshop with Slogan Car, San Francisco* 1988

76 | *Thanksgiving Service, Camp Roberts, California* 1942

77 | *Huge Class in Final Exam, University of California at Berkeley* 1947

78 | *Before Pearl Harbor, ROTC at Mission High School, San Francisco* 1938

79 | *Elephant Tour on Treasure Island (Golden Gate International Exhibition), San Francisco* 1939

80 | *Lunch Hour, San Francisco* 1934

81 | *Chinese Playground, San Francisco* 1938

82 | *High Hatter with Count Basie, San Francisco* 1939

83 | *Portrait of Count Basie, San Francisco* 1939

84 | *Indian High School Band, Arizona* 1937

85 | *Monster on Broadway, New York City* 1936

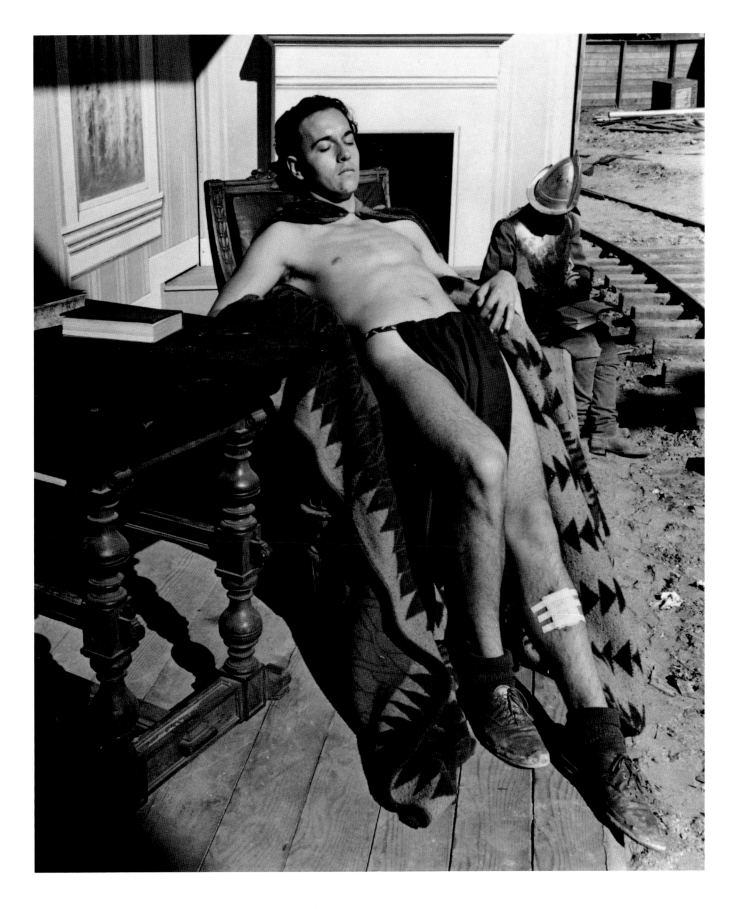

86 | *By the Railroad Track* 1939

87 | *Aerialists* 1939

88 | *Catastrophe* 1957

89 │ *"Alice from Dallas, World's Fattest Girl," San Francisco* 1940

90 | *Only Males at an Outdoor Cafe in Franco Spain, Segovia* 1957

91 | *Chief Monk and Novice of a Buddhist Temple, Yunnan Province, China* 1944

92 | *Kunming Canal, China* 1944

93 | *Pin-up Ladies and Chiang Kai-shek, Kunming, China* 1944

94 | *Beneath a Giant Guardian the Fortune Teller, Yunnan Province, China* 1945

95 | *Geisha Doll and Friend* 1939

96 | *The Jump* 1939

97 | *The Cry* 1939

98 | *Fernand Léger with Irene and "Composition with Parrots"* 1940

99 | *Self-Portrait with Lovebird* 1934

100 │ *"The End is at Hand," Hyde Park, London* 1970

Chronology

Note: Traveling exhibitions are designated by organizing institution only.

1905	Born in Breslau, Germany (now Wrocław, Poland).
1914–23	Attends Johannes Gymnasium, Breslau, Germany.
1923–27	Receives B.A., Staatliche Akademie für Kunst und Kunstgewerbe zu Breslau, Germany. Studies with Otto Müller.
1926	Meets Erich Heckel. Travels to London.
1926–27	Studies art and philosophy at Schlesische Friedrich Wilhelms Universität zu Breslau.
1927	Exhibits paintings at Schlesischer Künstlerbund and in *Junge Talente*, Museum der Bildeneden Künste, Breslau. Moves to Berlin.
1928	Receives M.A., Preussiches Schulkollegium für Höhere Erzichung, Berlin.
1928–31	Travels in Europe.
1929–30	Postgraduate studies at Humboldt Universität zu Berlin and Berliner Akademie der Bildeneden Künste.
1929–32	Solo exhibition of paintings and drawings, Gurlitt Gallery, Berlin (1931); included in Berliner Secession and Preussiche Akademie der Künste exhibitions. Teaches art at various schools in Berlin.
1933	Leaves Germany; begins to photograph. Signs contract as photojournalist with Presse-Foto, Berlin. Travels to San Francisco, California, via Panama Canal.
1934	Joins California Camera Club, San Francisco, to use their darkroom facilities; meets members of club, mostly of the Pictorialist school. Travels north along coast to British Columbia, Canada. Publishes photographs in international magazines.
1935	Solo exhibition of drawings and watercolors, Paul Elder Gallery, San Francisco.
1936	Begins teaching art part-time at San Francisco State College. Travels across United States. Ceases affiliation with Presse-Foto and begins work for Pix, Inc. Accepts numerous magazine assignments.
1937	Solo exhibition of drawings at San Francisco Museum of Art, and of drawings and paintings at Delphic Studios, New York.
1937–62	Photographs published in *Saturday Evening Post*, *Life*, *Time*, *Look*, *National Geographic*, *Coronet*, U.S. Camera Annuals, and other magazines and periodicals.
1938	Appointed Assistant Professor of Art, San Francisco State College. Solo exhibition of photographs, *Colorful America*, M.H. de Young Memorial Museum, San Francisco, which circulates nationally. Appointed Assistant Professor of Art, San Francisco State College; establishes studio courses and comprehensive scholarly course on the history of modern art.
1939	Exhibits in *Contemporary Art*, Golden Gate International Exposition, San Francisco. Meets and photographs Laszlo Moholy-Nagy.
1940	Meets and photographs Fernand Léger.
1941	Solo exhibition, *Wondrous World*, M.H. de Young Memorial Museum, San Francisco. Included in exhibition *Image of Freedom*, Museum of Modern Art, New York.
1942–43	Graduates from the Signal Corps Motion Picture School, Astoria, New York. Serves with U.S. Army Signal Corps as still and motion picture photographer.
1943–45	Serves in the China–Burma–India Theatre, U.S. Office of War Information, with the Psychological Warfare Team.
1946	Establishes a creative photography program at San Francisco State College.

1949   Produces documentary films *The Chinese Peasant Goes to Market* and *Journey to Kunming*. Marries artist Gerrie von Pribosic.

1949–63   Establishes international film program, Art Movies, at San Francisco State College.

1950   Postgraduate work at University of Mexico.

1955   Appointed full Professor of Art, San Francisco State College.

1957   Travels and photographs throughout Western Europe as well as Morocco.

1962–72   Little photographic work due to prolonged illness; continues teaching 1965–75.

1968   Honored for Distinguished Teaching by California State Colleges.

1970   Visits Berlin for the first time since 1933.

1972   Starts to reprint early negatives.

1973   Retires from full-time teaching; named Professor Emeritus at San Francisco State University (formerly San Francisco State College).

1974–97   Numerous solo exhibitions, for example: Light Gallery, New York (1974); San Francisco Museum of Modern Art (1976); Castelli Gallery, New York (1979, 1981, 1985, 1990); Fraenkel Gallery, San Francisco (1980, 1985, 1988, 1991, 1995); Museum of Photographic Arts, San Diego (1984); Art Gallery of Ontario (1985); Houston Center for Photography (1986); Museo Casa Natal de Jovellanos, Valencia, Spain (1989); San Francisco Museum of Modern Art (1989); Ehlers Caudill Gallery, Chicago (1993); Paul Kopelkin Gallery, Los Angeles (1995).

Photographs included in important invitational group exhibitions, for example: *Aesthetics of Graffiti*, San Francisco Museum of Modern Art (1978); *Amerika Fotografie 1920–1940*, Kunsthaus, Zürich (1979); *When Words Fail*, International Center of Photography, New York (1980); *Fleeting Gestures: Treasures of Dance Photography*, International Center of Photography, New York (1981); *American Images: Photography 1945–1980*, Barbican Centre, London (1985); *The Machine Age in America 1918–1941*, The Brooklyn Museum of Art (1986); *American Dreams*, Centro de Arte Reina Sofia, Madrid (1987); *On the Art of Fixing a Shadow: 150 Years of Photography*, National Gallery of Art, Washington, D.C. (1989).

1977   Awarded Guggenheim Fellowship in photography.

1979   Produces documentary film *Le Palais Idéal* (1983), edited by Karen Holmes.

1984   Publishes *The Restless Decade: John Gutmann's Photographs of the Thirties*, intro. by Max Kozloff, ed. Lew Thomas, New York (Abrams), reprinted in 1996.

1995   *Prelude to Photography*, M.H. de Young Memorial Museum, San Francisco, featured paintings and drawings done in Germany and America in the late 1920s and 1930s. Concurrent exhibition of drawings at 871 Fine Arts Gallery, San Francisco, and of vintage photographs and objects from Gutmann's collections, *Death*, at Fraenkel Gallery, San Francisco.

1997   Exhibition *John Gutmann: Parallels in Focus*, San Francisco State University, features photographs, paintings, drawings, films, and ephemera honoring Gutmann's career and contributions to the university.

1998   Dies, San Francisco, California.

Selected Bibliography: Catalogues and Collected Works

as i saw it: Photographs by John Gutmann, exhib. cat. by John
    Humphrey, San Francisco, San Francisco Museum of Modern Art,
    1976

Alain Dupuy, *John Gutmann 1933–1939*,
    Valencia (II Jornades Fotogràfiques a València) 1985

Gutmann, exhib. cat. by Maia-Mari Sutnik, Toronto,
    Art Gallery of Ontario, 1985

John Gutmann: A Selection of Unpublished Images,
    San Francisco (Zyzzyva, Inc.) 1987

John Gutmann: Beyond the Document , exhib. cat., San Francisco,
    San Francisco Museum of Modern Art, 1989

John Gutmann: 99 Photografias , America, 1934–1954,
    Barcelona (Fundacio Caixa de Pensions) 1989

John Gutmann, *Parallels in Focus Featuring the Original "Talking
    Pictures, "* San Francisco (San Francisco State University) 1997

Lew Thomas (ed.), *The Restless Decade: John Gutmann's Photographs
    of the Thirties*, intro. by Max Kozloff, New York (Abrams)
    1984, reprinted 1996